Say & Pray Easter

STICKER AND ACTIVITY BOOK

Diane Stortz

illustrated by **Sarah Ward**

Tommy NELSON®

An Imprint of Thomas Nelson
thomasnelson.com

Happy Easter!

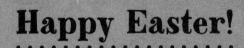

God sent His Son, Jesus, to show us His love. At Easter we see signs of new life, and we celebrate the new life Jesus gives.

Finish the picture with 4 stickers.

from Mark 10:13–16, Luke 2:52

Can you name these signs of Easter? Draw lines to match the pictures that are the same. Then trace the words.

cross

lily

bunny

chick

church

Jesus grew from a baby to a boy to a man.

Find the stickers that show how Jesus grew up.

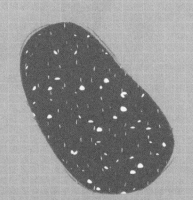

3

Jesus Our King

Jesus rode toward Jerusalem on a donkey colt. People put their coats on the road and waved palm branches to welcome Him. They praised God and shouted, "Hosanna! God saves!"

Jesus sent the disciples to find the donkey for Him to ride. Help the disciples bring the donkey colt and its mother to Jesus.

START

END

4

Finish the scene with the picture stickers.

Circle the picture with 2 donkeys. Add the sticker of the number 2.

Hosanna means "God saves."

Color the picture of the people praising God.

5

from Matthew 21:1–11

Jesus Our Healer

People who were hurt or sick came to the temple to see Jesus. People who were blind came. People who couldn't walk came. And Jesus healed them. Now they could see! Now they could walk!

Find the objects hidden in the picture.

bat   bug   book   ball   pencil   heart   envelope   flashlight   sock

Another time, Jesus made 10 sick men well, but only one came back to thank Him. Finish the picture with stickers. Then trace the number 10. Circle the man who said thank you.

10

Read and trace the words.

see

thank you

happy

walk

from Matthew 21:14–16, Luke 17:11–19

7

Jesus Our Teacher

Wherever Jesus went, people came to hear Him teach. He told them, "God is your Father. Love God and love one another."

Help the people find their way to the temple. Then place the sticker that shows who they are going to see.

START

from Matthew 6:25–34, 22:34–40; Luke 21:37–38

END

Use the stickers to finish the verse about God's most important rule.

Jesus answered, "Love the Lord your God with all your , soul and ."

—MATTHEW 22:37 ICB

Another time, Jesus said, "Don't worry about food and clothing. God knows what you need."

Find the missing stickers of food and clothing. Then circle the matching items.

An Evil Plan

The people loved Jesus. But the leaders were jealous of Him. Judas came to talk with the leaders. They gave Judas money to help them arrest Jesus in a quiet place.

Finish the scene with stickers.

Place the stickers of Judas and Jesus in the spaces to finish the sentence.

_____ was one of Jesus' disciples, but Judas was not a good friend to _____

Compare the pictures. Can you find 6 differences?

Finish the sentences by tracing the words.

Jesus always did right.

The leaders' plan was wrong.

from Matthew 21:14–15; Luke 22:1–6

11

Dinner with the Disciples

Jesus and the disciples ate the Passover dinner together. During the meal, Jesus shared bread and a drink with His friends. He said, "Do this to remember Me."

Add the stickers to name the objects in the picture.

Jesus had 12 disciples. Each one needs a plate! Add the missing plates and the number 12 sticker.

from Matthew 26:26–29, Luke 22:10–20, John 13:12–15

2 3
1
4
15

Connect the dots to complete
the picture of Jesus' meal.
Then color the picture.

14 5
13 6
12 7
11 8
10 9

Jesus told the disciples to
help and serve others.

Finish the picture with
stickers that show
children helping.

In the Garden

Jesus prayed about God's plan for Him.
Jesus asked three disciples to keep watch
while He prayed, but they fell asleep.

Finish the scene with the picture stickers. Then circle these items:

bat   tree   butterfly   fox   snail   flower

Add the stickers that name the activity. Then color the pictures.

Judas came to the garden with soldiers to arrest Jesus. Follow their path.

START

END

from Matthew 26:30, 36–56

15

Peter Is Afraid

The disciples ran away when Jesus was arrested. Peter followed the soldiers to see what would happen to Jesus. Peter said, "I don't know Jesus" three times, then a rooster crowed.

Circle the picture with 3 items. Add the sticker of the number 3.

from Matthew 26:56–58, 69–75; Luke 22:31–34

Finish the scene with the picture stickers. Then find these hidden objects:

ruler

flag

banana

key

hat

tie

Can you *cock-a-doodle-doo* like a rooster? Trace the words. Then match each animal with the sound it makes.

c o w

neigh

c a t

oink

p i g

moo

h o r s e

meow

A Long Night

Jesus did nothing wrong, but the leaders did not care. They said that Jesus should die. That night, they took Jesus to Pilate, a Roman ruler.

Find the stickers that show what happened to Jesus after He was arrested. Then follow the path.

START

1. Jesus was arrested.

2. The leaders lied about Jesus.

3. Pilate asked Jesus questions.

4. The people yelled at Pilate to kill Jesus.

END

Jesus would have to die on a cross. Soldiers told a man named Simon to help Jesus carry it. Connect the dots to complete the picture.

Some animals come out only at night.

Compare the pictures.
Can you find 5 differences?

from Matthew 27:1–2, 11–23, 32

The Saddest Day

Jesus died on a cross. Then two of His followers wrapped His body and placed it in a tomb carved in the rock. They closed the tomb with a large stone. Then soldiers stood guard.

Finish the picture with stickers.

**Connect the dots to draw Jesus' tomb.
Add the sticker of the stone that closed the tomb.
Then color the picture.**

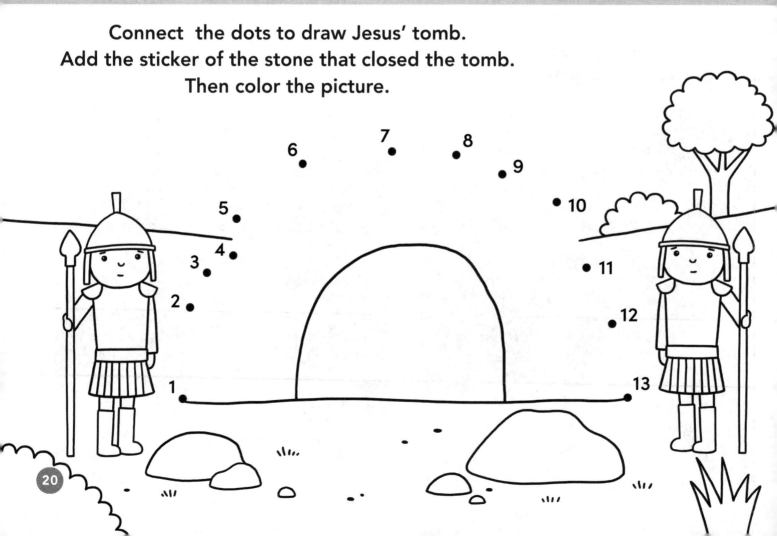

Use stickers to finish the verse.

 died to take
away our sins
as the ⬛ predicted.

—1 Corinthians 15:3 GW

Where Is Jesus?

Complete the story with the people stickers.

On the third day after Jesus died, an angel rolled the stone away from the tomb.

Women came to the tomb. The tomb was empty!

Mary ran to tell the disciples.
"Where could Jesus be?" she asked.

Peter and John ran to the tomb. They looked inside. The tomb was empty!

An angel said, "Jesus is not here. He has risen!"

Find the sticker of the empty tomb. Then circle the other items that are empty. Trace the word.

empty

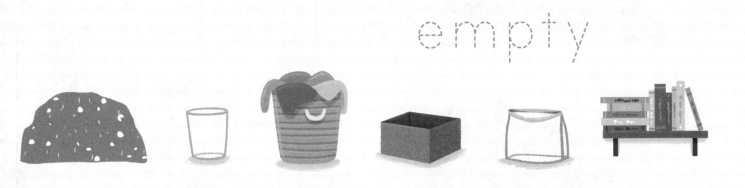

The guards fainted when they saw the angel. Help them go back to the city after they wake up.

END

START

23

from Matthew 28:1–7, 11; Luke 24:10; John 20:1–10

Jesus Is Alive!

Many of Jesus' friends saw Him after He rose from the dead. At different times, Jesus met a group of women, two travelers, and His disciples. How happy they all were!

Finish the picture with stickers.

Help the travelers hurry back to Jerusalem to tell the disciples that Jesus is alive.

START

END

24

Finish the scene with the picture stickers. Then circle these items:

chair   bowl   mouse   moon   cat

Add the word sticker that tells what the disciples said.

Jesus is ___ !

Breakfast with Jesus

Peter and some other disciples were fishing when they saw Jesus! He told them where to put down their nets, and they caught many fish. Then He said, "Come and have breakfast."

Compare the pictures. Can you find 5 differences?

Finish the pattern with stickers.

Peter caught 153 fish!

13

14

12

11

10

1

2

9

3

8

4

7

5

6

Connect the dots and add stickers to help Peter catch the fish.

Jesus forgave Peter for saying that he did not know Jesus. Peter was happy to be forgiven. Color the picture and trace the word.

happy

from John 21:1–17

Jesus Returns to Heaven

Jesus led the disciples to a hillside. They watched as Jesus went up in a cloud to return to heaven. Then two angels told the disciples, "One day Jesus will come back!"

Connect the dots. Then add the sticker that shows who the disciples are watching in the sky.

For each picture, circle whether it shows UP or DOWN.

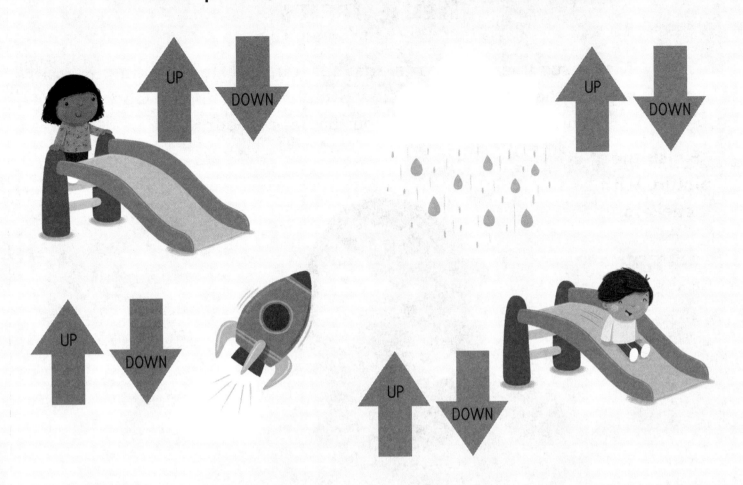

Finish the picture with stickers. Then write the numbers to answer the questions.

How many angels talked to the disciples? _____

How many disciples saw Jesus return to heaven? _____

from Acts 1:9–11

King Jesus

Now Jesus rules our hearts from heaven, and He is making a place there for all who follow Him. He helps us love God and each other. Jesus is our Savior and our King!

Finish the picture with stickers.

from John 14:1–7, Revelation 21:1–7, 10–21, 22:1–5

Jesus is in heaven now, but He hears us when we pray!

Finish the picture with stickers.

What special book tells us all about Jesus and how to live with Him forever? Find the sticker that names the book.

Read and trace the words. Then match each word to its picture. Color the pictures.

King

cross

heaven

Answers for spot-the-difference activities on pages 11, 19, and 26.

Say and Pray Bible Easter Sticker and Activity Book

© 2023 Diane Stortz

Tommy Nelson, PO Box 141000, Nashville, TN 37214

Published in Nashville, Tennessee, by Tommy Nelson. Tommy Nelson is an imprint of Thomas Nelson. Thomas Nelson is a registered trademark of HarperCollins Christian Publishing, Inc.

Published in association with the Books & Such Literary Management, attention: Janet Kobobel Grant, 52 Mission Circle, Suite 122 PMB 170, Santa Rosa, California 95409-5370, www.booksandsuch.com.

Tommy Nelson titles may be purchased in bulk for educational, business, fundraising, or sales promotional use. For information, please e-mail SpecialMarkets@ThomasNelson.com.

ISBN 978-1-4002-3923-8

Library of Congress Cataloging-in-Publication Data on file.

Illustrated by Sarah Ward

Printed in the United States
23 24 25 26 27 CWM 10 9 8 7 6 5 4 3 2 1

Mfr: CWM / Jefferson City, MO / December 2022 / PO # 12173939